# Police Officers

By Jacqueline Laks Gorman

Reading consultant: Susan Nations, M.Ed., author/literacy coach/consultant

**Gareth Stevens**
Publishing

Please visit our Web site www.garethstevens.com. For a free color catalog of all our high-quality books, call toll free 1-800-542-2595 or fax 1-877-542-2596.

Library of Congress Cataloging-in-Publication Data

Gorman, Jacqueline Laks, 1955-
 Police officer / by Jacqueline Laks Gorman.
  p. cm. — (People in my community)
  Summary: Explains what police officers do, including helping people in trouble, stopping people who break the law, and directing traffic.
  Includes bibliographical references and index.
  ISBN: 978-1-4339-3351-6 (pbk.)
  ISBN: 978-1-4339-3352-3 (6-pack)
  ISBN: 978-1-4339-3350-9 (library binding)
  1. Police—Juvenile literature. [1. Police.   2. Occupations.]   I. Title.
  HV7922.G67    2002
  363.2'2—dc21                                                    2002024622

New edition published 2010 by
**Gareth Stevens Publishing**
111 East 14th Street, Suite 349
New York, NY 10003

New text and images this edition copyright © 2010 Gareth Stevens Publishing

Original edition published 2003 by Weekly Reader® Books
An imprint of Gareth Stevens Publishing
Original edition text and images copyright © 2003 Gareth Stevens Publishing

Art direction: Haley Harasymiw, Tammy Gruenewald
Page layout: Michael Flynn, Katherine A. Goedheer
Editorial direction: Kerri O'Donnell, Diane Laska Swanke

Photo credits: Cover, back cover, p. 1 © Darrin Klimek/Digital Vision/Getty Images; pp. 5, 15 © Shutterstock.com; pp. 7, 9, 11, 13, 17, 19, 21 by Gregg Andersen.

Printed in the United States of America

CPSIA compliance information: Batch #WW10GS: For further information contact Gareth Stevens, New York, New York at 1-800-542-2595.

# Table of Contents

**Boldface** words appear in the glossary.

# An Important Job

A police officer has an important job. A police officer helps people.

A police officer helps people in trouble. A police officer helps keep people safe.

## Police Gear

Police officers wear **badges** and special **uniforms**. They use radios to talk to each other.

radio

# A Safe Neighborhood

Police officers stop people who break the **law**. They help keep your **neighborhood** safe.

Some police officers ride in police cars. Some ride on motorcycles.

**motorcycles**

Sometimes police officers direct traffic. They give tickets to drivers who drive too fast.

Sometimes police officers visit schools. They talk about how to stay safe.

If you are ever lost or need help, a police officer can help you.

Would you like to be a police officer?

# Glossary

**badge:** a small sign that identifies people and is pinned to their clothes

**law:** a rule that people follow

**neighborhood:** the streets and homes around the place you live

**uniform:** clothing worn by members of a group such as firefighters, mail carriers, or police officers

# For More Information

## Books

Bourgeois, Paulette. *Police Officers.*
    Toronto, ON: Kids Can Press, 2004.
Braithwaite, Jill. *Police Cars.*
    Minneapolis, MN: Lerner Publications, 2004.
Gorman, Jacqueline Laks. *Why Do We Have Laws?*
    New York: Gareth Stevens Publishing, 2008.
McMahon, Kara. *Police Officers!*
    New York: Random House, 2006.

## Web Sites

**Free Police and Safety Coloring and Activity Pages**
http://kids.askacop.org/coloringpages.html

# Index

## About the Author

**Jacqueline Laks Gorman** is a writer and editor. She grew up in New York City and began her career working on encyclopedias and other reference books. Since then, she has worked on many different kinds of books. She lives with her husband and children, Colin and Caitlin, in DeKalb, Illinois.